Wee Sing®

ANIMALS, ANIMALS, ANIMALS

By
Pamela Conn Beall and
Susan Hagen Nipp

Illustrated by
Nancy Spence Klein

PSS!
PRICE STERN SLOAN

To all who delight in animals

Special thanks to the Wee Singers:

Kiah Beehler, Aaron Comfort, Beth Dyer,
Sarah Dyer, Barry Hagen, Mauri Macy,
Sherry Macy, Jay Miller, Dallas McKennon,
Karley Molzahn, and Marcus Varner,
and to our musical producers and arrangers,
Barry Hagen and Mauri Macy.

Thanks also to Hilary Beall, Kyle Beall,
Lindsay Beall, Emily Boucher, Monique Conn,
Randy Conn, Linda Dobbeck, Kirsten Groener,
Marika Groener, Sylvia Groener, Allison Hagen,
McKenzie Hagen, Catherine Klein, Erin Klein,
Sam Klein, John Macy, Peter Macy, Rachel Macy,
Devin Nipp, Ryan Nipp, Heather Rodgers,
and Rory Rodgers.

The Snake © 1999 Pamela Conn Beall, Susan Hagen Nipp. *The Swan;
Ladybug; The Caterpillar; The Snail; Raccoon Has a Bushy Tail; Goin' to the
Zoo; The Lion; Animals; Animal Action* © 1999 Pamela Conn Beall. *Animals,
Animals; The Mosquito; The Hippopotamus and the Rhinoceros; The Ostrich;
The Giraffe; The Animal Parade* © 1999 Susan Hagen Nipp.

Printed on recycled paper

Typesetting and engraving by Charles Gravenhorst, ProScore Music Engraving

ISBN: 0-8431-4933-7

REFACE

"With a moo, moo here, and a moo, moo there . . ." MacDonald had a farm, E-I-E-I-O!" "Baa, baa, black sheep, have you any wool?". . . "The eentsy, weentsy spider went up the water spout". . . Sound familiar? Learning about animals, the sounds they make, and how they move is a basic yet joyful part of learning during early childhood.

Some of the first sounds a toddler makes are those of familiar pets or farm animals. From hopping like a rabbit to galloping like a horse, mimicking the movement of animals is not only fun, but is a natural way to learn basic body movements. Caring for family pets helps teach children responsibility. While watching a spider spin a web or a bird catch a worm, a child learns about the food chain. Seeing a chick peck its way out of a shell is an introduction to understanding the cycle of life.

In *Wee Sing Animals, Animals, Animals,* we have included songs, poems and fingerplays about a variety of animals most familiar to children. Some are silly, some are informational, and many are full of action to encourage movement. All of them are fun for singing or chanting along.

We hope you enjoy this musical journey as we meet animals on the farm, at the pond, in the garden, in the air, in the forest, and at the zoo.

Pam Beall
Susan Nipp

TABLE OF CONTENTS

IN THE AIR

IN THE FOREST

AT THE ZOO

Titles in italics are poems.
*Titles with asterisks are fingerplays.

ANIMALS, ANIMALS

Susan Nipp   *Susan Nipp*

Descant

An - i-mals, an - i-mals,   an - i-mals, an - i-mals,

Chorus *(continue descant)*

An - i-mals are big,   an - i - mals are small,

An - i-mals can walk   and   fly   and swim and crawl,

An - i-mals are spe-cial,   u - nique and col - or-ful,

An - i-mals of ev - 'ry kind are   all   so won-der-ful.

(descant ending)

An - i-mals,   an - i-mals,   I love an - i-mals.

Verse

1. A cow is a mam mal,_ a trout is a fish,_ A

bee-tle is an in sect,_ I'll tell you more than this, A

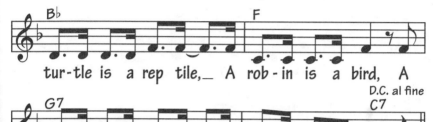

tur-tle is a rep tile,_ A rob-in is a bird, A

D.C. al fine

frog is an am-phib-i-an, I love to say each word.

2. A whale is a mammal, a shark is a fish,
   A bee is an insect, I'll tell you more than this,
   A snake is a reptile, a penguin is a bird,
   A toad is an amphibian, I love to say each word.
   (repeat descant and chorus)

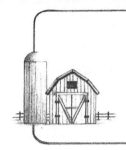

On the Farm

OLD MACDONALD HAD A FARM

Traditional

1. Old Mac-Don-ald had a farm, E - I - E - I - O!

And on his farm he had some chicks, E - I - E - I - O!

With a ⒶChick, chick here, and a chick, chick there,

Here a chick, there a chick, Ev'ry-where a chick, chick,

Old Mac-Don-ald had a farm, E - I - E - I - O!

2. And on his farm he had some ducks, E-I-E-I-O!
   With a ⒷQuack, quack here, and a quack, quack there,
   Here a quack, there a quack, ev'rywhere a quack, quack,
   Ⓐ Chick, chick here, and a chick, chick there,
   Here a chick, there a chick, ev'rywhere a chick, chick,
   Old MacDonald had a farm, E-I-E-I-O!

3. . . . cow . . . Ⓒ moo, moo . . .
4. . . . turkey . . . Ⓓ gobble, gobble . . .
5. . . . pig . . . Ⓔ oink, oink . . .
6. . . . donkey . . . Ⓕ hee-haw . . .

Actions:
Ⓐ Bob head
Ⓑ Flap elbows
Ⓒ Milk cow
Ⓓ Make turkey tail by hooking
   thumbs and spreading fingers
Ⓔ Push up tip of nose
Ⓕ Hands up on head to make ears

ANIMAL SONG

"Quack, quack," says the duck,
"Meow, meow," says the cat,
"Caw, caw," says the crow,
"Squeak, squeak," says the rat.

"Tu-whoo," says the owl,
"Bow-wow," says the dog,
"Moo, moo," says the cow,
"Grunt, grunt," says the hog.

A fine song they sing
With voices so clear,
It's really quite nice
And lovely to hear.

Traditional, adapted

9

SIX LITTLE DUCKS

Traditional

1. Six lit-tle ducks that I once knew,
Fat ones, skin-ny ones, fair ones, too, But the
one lit-tle duck with the feath-er on his back,
He led the oth-ers with a quack, quack, quack!
Quack, quack, quack, quack, quack, quack!
He led the oth-ers with a quack, quack, quack!

2. Down to the river they would go,
   Wibble wobble, wibble wobble, to and fro,
   But the one little duck with the feather on his back,
   He led the others with a quack, quack, quack!
   Quack, quack, quack, quack, quack, quack!
   He led the others with a quack, quack, quack!

3. Home from the river they would come,
   Wibble wobble, wibble wobble, ho-hum-hum! . .

LITTLE PETER RABBIT

(Tune: Battle Hymn)

Traditional

1. Lit-tle Pe-ter Rab-bit had a fly up-on his ear,

Lit-tle Pe-ter Rab-bit had a fly up-on his ear,

Lit-tle Pe-ter Rab-bit had a fly up-on his ear,

And he flicked it 'til it flew a - way.

2. Do not sing "Rabbit" but do action.
3. Do not sing "Rabbit" and "fly," but do actions.
4. Do not sing "Rabbit," "fly," and "ear," but do actions.

Actions:
Ⓐ Hands make rabbit ears Ⓑ Fingers fly away
Ⓒ Point to ear Ⓓ Flick ear

GOBBLE, GOBBLE
(Fingerplay)

A turkey is a funny bird,
*(make turkey tail by hooking thumbs
and spreading fingers)*
His head goes wobble, wobble,
(shake head from side to side)
And he knows just one word,
(hold up one finger)
Gobble, gobble, gobble.
(shake head, sound like turkey)

11

FIVE LITTLE CHICKENS

Said the first little chicken
With a slight little squirm,
"Oh, I wish I could find
A fat little worm!"

Said the next little chicken
With an odd little shrug,
"Oh, I wish I could find
A fat little bug!"

Said the third little chicken
With a sharp little squeal,
"Oh, I wish I could find
Some nice yellow meal!"

Said the fourth little chicken
With a small sigh of grief,
"Oh, I wish I could find
A green little leaf!"

Said the fifth little chicken
With a faint little moan,
"Oh, I wish I could find
A wee gravel stone!"

"Now, see here," said the mother
From the green garden patch,
"If you want any breakfast,
You must come and scratch."

Anonymous

12

BAA, BAA, BLACK SHEEP

Traditional

Baa, baa, black sheep, have you an-y wool?

Yes, sir, yes, sir, three bags full;

One for my mas-ter, one for my dame, And

one for the lit-tle boy who lives down the lane.

SWEETLY SINGS THE DONKEY
(Round)

Traditional

Sweet-ly sings the don-key At the break of day;

If you do not feed him, This is what he'll say:

"Hee-haw! Hee-haw! Hee-haw, hee-haw, hee-haw!"

TINGALAYO

Traditional West Indies

Chorus

F C G7 C

Tin-ga-lay-o! *(clap, clap)* Come, lit-tle don-key, come,_

F C G7 C **Fine**

Tin-ga-lay-o! *(clap, clap)* Come, lit-tle don-key, come._

Verse

F C

1. M' don-key walk, m' don-key talk, M' don-key

G7 C F

eat with a knife and fork, M' don-key walk, m'

D.C. al fine

C G7 C

don-key talk, M' don-key eat with a knife and fork.

2. M'donkey eat, m'donkey sleep,
   M'donkey kick with his two hind feet.
   M'donkey eat, m'donkey sleep,
   M'donkey kick with his two hind feet.
   Tingalayo! Come, little donkey, come,
   Tingalayo! Come, little donkey, come.

14

THE OLD GRAY MARE

Adapted Spiritual

1. The old gray mare, she ain't what she used to be,

Ain't what she used to be, ain't what she used to be,

The old gray mare, she ain't what she used to be,

Man-y long years a - go.   Man-y long years a - go,

Man-y long years a - go.   The old gray mare, she

ain't what she used to be, Man-y long years a - go.

2. The old gray mare, she kicked on the whiffletree*,
   Kicked on the whiffletree, kicked on the whiffletree,
   The old gray mare, she kicked on the whiffletree,
   Many long years ago.
   Many long years ago, Many long years ago,
   The old gray mare, she kicked on the whiffletree,
   Many long years ago.

* crossbar at the front of a wagon to
  which the harness strings are attached

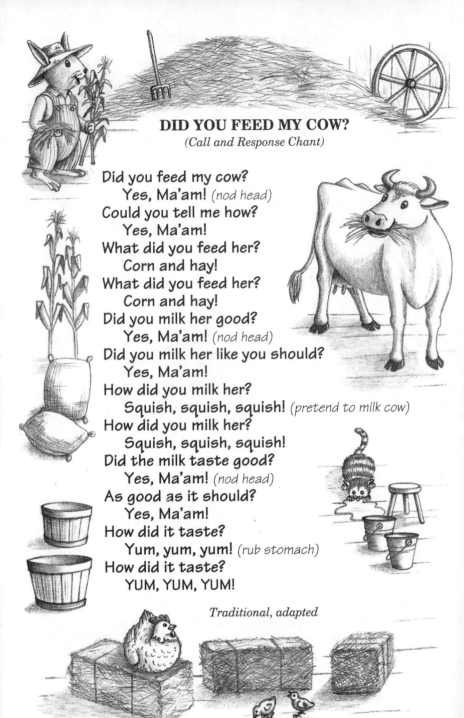

DID YOU FEED MY COW?
(Call and Response Chant)

Did you feed my cow?
   Yes, Ma'am! *(nod head)*
Could you tell me how?
   Yes, Ma'am!
What did you feed her?
   Corn and hay!
What did you feed her?
   Corn and hay!
Did you milk her good?
   Yes, Ma'am! *(nod head)*
Did you milk her like you should?
   Yes, Ma'am!
How did you milk her?
   Squish, squish, squish! *(pretend to milk cow)*
How did you milk her?
   Squish, squish, squish!
Did the milk taste good?
   Yes, Ma'am! *(nod head)*
As good as it should?
   Yes, Ma'am!
How did it taste?
   Yum, yum, yum! *(rub stomach)*
How did it taste?
   YUM, YUM, YUM!

Traditional, adapted

16

BILL GROGAN'S GOAT

Traditional

1. There was a man,___ Now please take note,___ There was a man,___ Who had a goat,___ He loved that goat,___ In-deed he did,_ He loved that goat, Just like a kid.___

(echo) (echo) (echo) (echo) (echo) (echo) (echo)

2. One day that goat *(echo each phrase)*
   Felt frisk and fine . . .
   Ate three red shirts . . .
   Right off the line . . .
   The man, he grabbed . . .
   Him by the back . . .
   And tied him to . . .
   A railroad track . . .

3. Now, when that train . . .
   Hove into sight . . .
   That goat grew pale . . .
   And green with fright . . .
   He heaved a sigh . . .
   As if in pain . . .
   Coughed up those shirts . . .
   And flagged the train . . .

17

THREE LITTLE PIGGIES

A. S. Gatty, Adapted　　　　　　　　　　　*Traditional*

1. A jol-ly old sow once lived in a sty, And

three lit - tle pig - gies had she. She

wad-dled a-bout, say-ing, "Oink, oink, oink,"

While the lit - tle ones said, "Wee, wee!"

2. Then one day one of the three little pigs,
   To her two little brothers, said she,
   "Why don't we ever go, 'Oink, oink, oink?'
   It's so childish to say, 'Wee, wee!'"

3. The three little piggies, they tried and they tried,
   And finally they could see
   That they weren't big enough to go, "Oink, oink, oink!"
   So they happily said, "Wee, wee!"

BINGO

Traditional

1. There was a farm-er had a dog and Bin-go was his

name-o.   B - I - N - G - O,   B - I - N - G - O,

B - I - N - G - O, and Bin-go was his name-o.

2. ... (Clap)-I-N-G-O ...   5. ... (X)-(X)-(X)-(X)-O ...
3. ... (X)-(X)-N-G-O ...   6. ... (X)-(X)-(X)-(X)-(X) ...
4. ... (X)-(X)-(X)-G-O ...

I LOVE LITTLE KITTY

Traditional

1. I__ love lit-tle kit-ty, her coat is so warm, And_

if I don't hurt her, she'll do me no harm. I'll_

sit by the fire_ and give her some food, And_

kit - ty will love me be - cause I am good.

2. I'll pat pretty kitty and then she will purr,
   And thus show her thanks for my kindness to her.
   So I'll not pull her tail nor drive her away,
   But kitty and I very gently will play.

BOUGHT ME A CAT

Southern U.S.

1. Bought me a cat and the cat pleased me, I fed my cat un-der yon-der tree. Cat goes fid-dle-i - fee.___

2. Bought me a hen and the hen pleased me, I fed my hen un-der yon-der tree. Hen goes chim-my-chuck, chim-my-chuck, Cat goes fid-dle-i - fee.___

3. Bought me a duck and the duck pleased me,
   I fed my duck under yonder tree.
   Duck goes quack, quack,
   Hen goes chimmy-chuck, chimmy-chuck,
   Cat goes fiddle-i-fee.

4. . . . Goose goes hissy, hissy . . .

5. . . . Sheep goes baa, baa . . .

6. . . . Pig goes oink, oink . . .

7. . . . Cow goes moo, moo . . .

8. . . . Horse goes neigh, neigh . . .

9. . . . Dog goes bow-wow, bow-wow . . .

At the Pond

FIVE LITTLE DUCKS
(Tune: Mulberry Bush)

Traditional

F

1. Five lit - tle ducks went out to play

C7

O - ver the hill and far a - way,

F

Moth-er Duck said,"Quack, quack, quack, quack,"

C7   F

But on - ly four lit - tle ducks came back.

2. Four little ducks . . .

3. Three little ducks . . .

4. Two little ducks . . .

5. One little duck . . .
But no little ducks came back.

6. So — Mother Duck said,
(*spoken*) "QUACK, QUACK, QUACK, QUACK,
QUACK, QUACK, QUACK, QUACK!"
And five little ducks came running back.

22

I CAUGHT A FISH

One, two, three, four, five,
Once I caught a fish alive;
Six, seven, eight, nine, ten,
Then I let him go again.

Why did you let him go?
Because he bit my finger so;
Which finger did he bite?
The little finger on the right.

Traditional

FIVE LITTLE FISHIES
(Fingerplay)

Five little fishies swimming in a pool,
(wiggle five fingers)

First one said, "The pool is cool."
(one finger up) (wrap arms around body)

Second one said, "The pool is deep."
(two fingers up) (hands measure deep)

Third one said, "I want to sleep."
(three fingers up) (rest head on hands)

Fourth one said, "Let's dive and dip."
(four fingers up) (hand dives and dips)

Fifth one said, "I spy a ship."
(five fingers up) (peer out under hand)

Fisherman's boat comes,
(fingers form V and move away from body)

Line goes ker-splash,
(pantomime throwing fishing line)

Away the five little fishies dash.
(wiggle five fingers away)

THE SWAN

Pam Beall   *Pam Beall*

Bb   Cm
Grace-ful   and   el - e - gant   swan

F7   Bb
Float-ing   a - round   on   the   pond,

Cm
Long   neck   and   feath-ers   so   white,

F7   Bb
You   make   a   beau - ti - ful   sight.

THE TURTLE
(Fingerplay)

This is my turtle, he lives in a shell;
(make fist) (cover fist with other hand)

It covers him snugly and fits him well.
(move fist up and down)

He pokes his head out when he wants to eat.
(extend pointer finger)

And pulls it back in when he wants to sleep.
(pull back pointer finger)

24

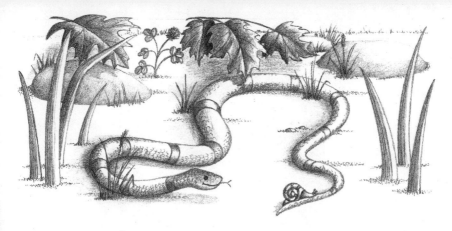

THE SNAKE

Susan Nipp, Pam Beall   *Traditional*

A slith-er-y, slip-per-y snake Was slith-er-ing

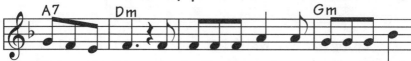

down to the lake, A fat lit-tle snail crept up on his tail,

Which made a nice lunch for the snake. *Gulp!*

CACKLE, CACKLE

Cackle, cackle, Madam Goose!
Have you any feathers loose?

Yes, I have, my little fellow,
Half enough to fill a pillow;

Here are quills, take one or ten
And make each one into a pen.

Traditional, adapted

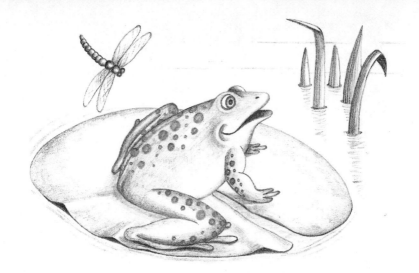

LITTLE GREEN FROG

Traditional

"Gung, gung," went the lit-tle green frog one day.

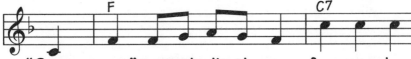

"Gung, gung," went the lit - tle green frog.

"Gung, gung," went the lit-tle green frog one day,

And his ⒶFingers eyes went, Ⓑ "aah, aah, gung."

Actions:
Ⓐ Fingers around eyes
Ⓑ Stick out tongue

THE MOSQUITO

Susan Nipp

Susan Nipp

Zzz - zt! (clap) Zzz - zt! (clap) Zzz -

zt! (clap, clap) Zzz - zt! (clap) Zzz - zt! (clap)

Zzz - zt! (clap, clap) zt! (clap) GOTCHA!

The mos-qui-to bites and it both-ers me 'cause it

itch, itch, itch-es all the night. (scratch, scratch) He's a

ti-ny bug but he both-ers me 'cause I

scratch, scratch, scratch his lit-tle bite. (scratch, scratch)

In the Garden

MISTER RABBIT

Spiritual

1. "Mis-ter Rab-bit, Mis-ter Rab-bit, your ears might-y long." "Yes, in - deed, they're put on wrong." Ev - 'ry lit - tle soul must shine, shine, shine,_ Ev - 'ry lit - tle soul must shine,_ shine, shine.

2. "Mister Rabbit, Mister Rabbit, your coat's mighty gray."
"Yes, indeed, 'twas made that way." . . .

3. "Mister Rabbit, Mister Rabbit, your nose always twitches."
"Yes, indeed, because it itches." . . .

4. "Mister Rabbit, Mister Rabbit, your tail's mighty white."
"Yes, indeed, I'm hoppin' out of sight." . . .

LADYBUG
(Tune: Pat-A-Cake)

Pam Beall   *Traditional*

Ⓐ La-dy-bug, la-dy-bug, where will you land?

Ⓑ La-dy-bug, la-dy-bug, Ⓒ come to my hand,

Ⓓ Then you can crawl all the way up my arm, And

Ⓔ I will as-sure you I'll do you no harm, When

Ⓕ you fly a-way, When you fly a-way, I

Ⓖ hope that you'll come back an-oth-er fine day.

Actions:

Ⓐ Flutter fingers while moving hand in air
Ⓑ Hold out palm of other hand
Ⓒ Land fluttering fingers in outstretched palm
Ⓓ Crawl fingers up arm
Ⓔ Gently shake finger while looking at arm
Ⓕ Flutter fingers of one hand from
   outstretched palm of other hand
Ⓖ Hold hand over heart while looking up

BABY BUMBLEBEE

Traditional

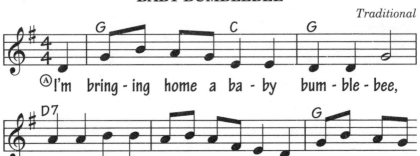

Ⓐ I'm bring-ing home a ba - by bum - ble - bee,

Won't my mom-my be so proud of me, I'm bring-ing home a

ba - by bum - ble - bee, Ⓑ OUCH! It stung me!

Actions:

Ⓐ Cup one hand over the other

Ⓑ Throw hands open

HERE IS THE BEEHIVE
(Fingerplay)

Here is the beehive, where are the bees?
(fist with thumb enclosed to make hive)
Hidden away where nobody sees.
(place other hand over the hive)
Watch and you'll see them come out of the hive,
(closely watch hive)
One, two, three, four, five.
*(very slowly, beginning with thumb,
fingers come out of hive one by one)*
Bzzzzzzz . . .
(all fly away)

NOBODY LIKES ME

Traditional

1. No - bod - y likes me, Ev - 'ry - bod - y hates me,

Guess I'll go eat worms, Long, thin, slim - y ones,

Short, fat, juic-y ones, It-sy, bit-sy, fuz-zy wuz-zy worms.

2. Down goes the first one,
   Down goes the second one,
   Oh, how they wiggle and squirm,
   Long, thin, slimy ones,
   Short, fat, juicy ones,
   Itsy, bitsy, fuzzy wuzzy worms.

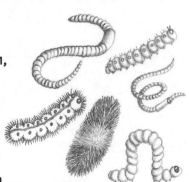

3. Up comes the first one,
   Up comes the second one,
   Oh, how they wiggle and squirm . . .

31

GRASSHOPPER

(Tune: Battle Hymn)

Traditional

1. The first grass-hop-per jumped right

o-ver the sec-ond grass-hop-per's back, Oh, the

first grass-hop-per jumped right o-ver the

sec-ond grass-hop-per's back, The first grass-hop-per

jumped right o-ver the sec-ond grass-hop-per's

back, Oh, the first grass-hop-per jumped right

o-ver the sec-ond grass-hop-per's back.

Chorus

They__were on-ly play-ing leap - frog,

They__were on-ly play-ing leap - frog,

32

They___were on - ly play - ing leap - frog,

When the first grass - hop - per jumped right

o - ver the sec - ond grass - hop - per's back.

2. One fleafly flew up the flue and
   the other fleafly flew down . . . *(4 times)*
   They were only playing fluefly . . . *(3 times)*
   When one fleafly flew up the flue and
   the other fleafly flew down.

THE CATERPILLAR
(Fingerplay)

I saw a fuzzy caterpillar
  (stroke pointer finger)
Crawling on the ground.
  (wiggle pointer finger)
Then, before I knew it,
  (elbows at sides, hands out)
He was nowhere to be found.
  (shake head)

I searched for him, but he was gone.
  (hand shading eyes, look from side to side)
I asked my mother, "Why?"
  (elbows at sides, hands out)
She said that he was resting
  (palms together at side of face)
To become a butterfly.
  (arms make flying motion)

Pam Beall

EENTSY, WEENTSY SPIDER

Traditional

Ⓐ The een - tsy, ween - tsy spi - der went up the wa - ter-spout. Ⓑ Down came the rain and Ⓒ washed the spi - der out. Ⓓ Out came the sun and Ⓔ dried up all the rain, And the Ⓐ een - tsy, ween - tsy spi - der went up the spout a - gain.

Actions:

Ⓐ Make circles out of thumbs and forefingers, put tips together, twist upward
Ⓑ Wiggle fingers while moving downward
Ⓒ Push outward
Ⓓ Make big circle with arms over head
Ⓔ Hands in front, palms up, move up in rhythm

THE SNAIL
(Tune: Twinkle, Twinkle)

Pam Beall   *Traditional*

Ⓐ Slow-ly__ creep-ing ti-ny snail, As you pull your pret-ty shell. Ⓑ Put your lit-tle feel-ers out, Ⓒ Move them as you look a-bout, Ⓓ Then_ go_ back in-to your shell Where you hide so ver-y well.

Actions:

Ⓐ Down on forearms and knees, creep like a snail

Ⓑ Pointer fingers on head like feelers

Ⓒ Move "feelers" and look around

Ⓓ Tuck head and arms close to body

35

THE BOLL WEEVIL

Southern Ballad

1. The boll wee-vil is a___ lit-tle black bug,

Come from Mex-i-co they say, Come all the way

to___ Tex-as, Just a-look-in' for a place to stay,

Just a-look-in' for a home,___ *(echo)*

Just a look-in' for a home.___ *(echo)*

2. The first time I saw the boll weevil,
   He was sittin' on the square;
   The next time I saw the boll weevil,
   He had all of his family there,
   Just a-lookin' for a home, *(echo)*
   Just a-lookin' for a home. *(echo)*

THE ANTS GO MARCHING

(Tune: When Johnny Comes Marching)

Traditional

1. The ants go march-ing one by one, Hur-rah,__

Hur - rah,__ The ants go march-ing one by one,

Hur - rah,__ Hur - rah,__ The ants go march-ing

one by one, The lit-tle one stops to suck his thumb

and they all go march-ing down__ to the ground__

to get out__ of the rain, Boom! Boom! Boom!

2. ... two ... tie his shoe ...
3. ... three ... climb a tree ...
4. ... four ... shut the door ...
5. ... five ... take a dive ...
6. ... six ... pick up sticks ...
7. ... seven ... pray to heaven ...
8. ... eight ... shut the gate ...
9. ... nine ... check the time ...
10. ... ten ... say, "THE END!"

In the Air

UP, UP IN THE SKY

Traditional

ⒶUp, up in the sky, the lit - tle birds fly, Down,Ⓑdown in their nest,_ the lit - tle birds rest. With a Ⓒwing on their left and a Ⓓwing on their right, We'll Ⓔlet the dear bird-ies sleep all through the night. ⒻShhh! They're Ⓔsleep-ing! TheⒼbright sun comes up, the Ⓗdew falls a - way, "Good

"①morn-ing, good morn-ing," the lit-tle birds say.

Actions:

Ⓐ Arms and hands flutter like wings
Ⓑ Arms form cradle in front, rock back and forth
Ⓒ Tuck left hand under left armpit
Ⓓ Tuck right hand under right armpit
Ⓔ Palms together at side of tilted head
Ⓕ Finger to lips
Ⓖ Arms make circle above head
Ⓗ Fingers flutter downward
① Bob head up and down

TWO LITTLE BLACKBIRDS
(Fingerplay)

Two little blackbirds
Sitting on a hill,
  (pointer fingers up)

One named Jack
  (one hand forward)

And one named Jill.
  (other hand forward)

Fly away, Jack,
  (one hand behind back)

Fly away, Jill.
  (other hand behind back)

Come back, Jack,
  (return one hand)

Come back, Jill.
  (return other hand)

39

LITTLE BIRD

Traditional, Adapted

Once I ⒜saw a lit-tle bird come ⒝hop, hop, hop;

So I ⒞cried, "Lit-tle bird, won't you ⒟stop, stop, stop?"

I was ⒠go-ing to the win-dow to say, ⒡"How do you do?"

But he ⒢shook his lit-tle tail and far a-⒣way he flew.

Actions:

ⒶHands shade eyes　ⒷHop three times　ⒸHands cupped around mouth
ⒹPush hands out in front　ⒺThree steps forward
ⒻWave hand　ⒼWiggle backside　ⒽFlap arms

LITTLE JENNY WREN

As little Jenny Wren
Was sitting by her shed,
She waggled with her tail
And nodded with her head.

She waggled with her tail
And nodded with her head,
As little Jenny Wren
Was sitting by the shed.

Traditional

KOOKABURRA

(Round)

Traditional

1. Kook-a-bur-ra sits in the old gum tree,___

Mer-ry, mer-ry king of the bush is he,___

Laugh, Kook-a-bur-ra, laugh, Kook-a-bur-ra,

Gay your life must be.

2. Kookaburra sits in the old gum tree
   Eating all the gumdrops he can see,
   Stop, Kookaburra, stop, Kookaburra,
   Leave some there for me.

THE OWL

There was an old owl who lived in an oak,
The more he heard, the less he spoke;
The less he spoke, the more he heard.
Why aren't we all like that wise old bird?

Traditional

41

THREE BLUE PIGEONS

Traditional

1. Three blue pi-geons sitting on a wall,

Three blue pi - geons_ sitting on a wall.

One flew a - way! O - o - oh.

2. Two blue pigeons sitting on a wall,
   Two blue pigeons sitting on a wall,
   Another flew away! O-o-oh.

3. One blue pigeon sitting on a wall . . .
   And the third flew away! O-o-oh.

4. No blue pigeons sitting on a wall . . .
   One flew back! Whee-ee-ee!

5. One blue pigeon sitting on a wall . . .
   Another flew back! Whee-ee-ee!

6. Two blue pigeons sitting on a wall . . .
   And the third flew back! Whee-ee-ee!

7. Three blue pigeons sitting on a wall,
   Three blue pigeons sitting on a wall.

Suggestion: Act out the words.

THE OLD MAN

There was an old man with a beard,
Who said, "It is just as I feared!
Two owls and a hen,
Four larks and a wren,
Have all built their nests in my beard!"

Edward Lear

42

THE CUCKOO

Traditional

Oh, I went to the flow-ing stream and_
what did I hear? From the qui - et wood
came the sound of the cuck-oo so clear.

Chorus

Ho - li - ah, Ho - le-rah - ki - ki - ah,
ho - le-rah, cuck-oo, Ho - le-rah-ki - ki-ah,
ho - le-rah, cuck-oo, Ho - le-rah - ki - ki-ah,
ho-le-rah, cuck-oo, Ho-le-rah-ki-ki-ah, Oh!

Actions:

Ho-li-ah: rapidly slap knees

Ho-le-rah-ki-ki-ah: slap knees, clap hands, snap fingers
(continue throughout chorus)

In the Forest

SQUIRREL, SQUIRREL

Traditional

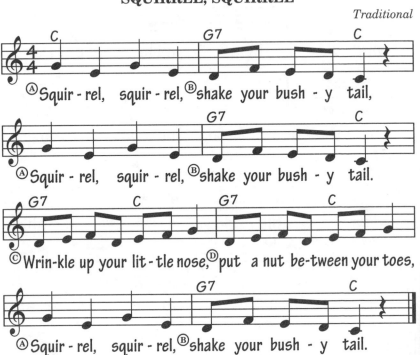

Ⓐ Squir - rel, squir - rel, Ⓑ shake your bush - y tail,

Ⓐ Squir - rel, squir - rel, Ⓑ shake your bush - y tail.

Ⓒ Wrin-kle up your lit - tle nose, Ⓓ put a nut be-tween your toes,

Ⓐ Squir - rel, squir - rel, Ⓑ shake your bush - y tail.

Actions:

Ⓐ Standing, knees bent, elbows bent, hands cupped, fingers down
Ⓑ Wiggle backside
Ⓒ Push up nose with pointer finger
Ⓓ Elbows bent, hands make fists, put fists together

THE LITTLE SKUNK'S HOLE
(Tune: Turkey in the Straw)

Traditional

1. Oh, I stuck my head in the lit-tle skunk's hole,

And the lit-tle skunk said, "Well, bless my soul!

Take it out! Take it out! Take it out! Re-move it!"

2. Oh, I didn't take it out,
   And the little skunk said,
   "If you don't take it out,
   You'll wish you had,
   Take it out! Take it out!"
   Pheew! I removed it!

RABBIT AIN'T GOT NO TAIL
(Tune: Mary Had a Little Lamb)

Traditional

Rab-bit ain't got no tail at all, Tail at all, tail at all,

Rab-bit ain't got no tail at all, Just a pow-der puff.

Suggestion: Repeat several times singing faster and faster.

RACCOON HAS A BUSHY TAIL

Adapted, Pam Beall *Traditional*

Chorus

Rac-coon has a bush-y tail, Pos-sum's tail is bare, Rab-bit ain't got no tail at all, Just a lit-tle bit-ty bunch of hair.

Verse

1. Rac-coon is a clev-er thing, Ram-blin' in the dark, You should see him run a-way When he hears old Ro-ver bark.

2. Possum's like a big old rat
   Wandrin' through the town,
   Climbed up in a 'simmon tree*
   Where he's hangin' upside down.
   (chorus after each verse)

3. Rabbit wears a furry coat,
   Likes to run and play,
   If you try to get too close,
   He'll hop, hop, hop away.

* persimmon tree

46

LITTLE BUNNY FOO FOO
(Tune: Down by the Station)

Traditional

1. Lit-tle Bun-ny Foo Foo, hop-pin' through the for-est,

Scoop-in' up the field mice and bop-pin' 'em on the head.

(Spoken) **Down came the good fairy — And she said:**

"Lit-tle Bun-ny Foo Foo, I don't want to see you

Scoop-in' up the field mice and bop-pin' 'em on the head."

(Spoken)

"I'll give you *three* chances, and if you don't behave,
I'll turn you into a goon!" The next day:

2. Little Bunny Foo Foo, hoppin' through the forest . . .
   "I'll give you *two* more chances . . . "

3. . . . "I'll give you *one* more chance . . . "

4. . . . "I gave you three chances and you didn't behave.
   Now you're a goon! POOF!"

The moral of the story is:
HARE TODAY, GOON TOMORROW

47

THE BEAR WENT OVER THE MOUNTAIN

Traditional

1. The bear went o-ver the moun-tain, The

bear went o-ver the moun-tain, The bear went

o-ver the moun-tain To see what he could see.

Chorus

To see what he could see, To see what he could see,

2. The other side of the mountain,
   The other side of the mountain,
   The other side of the mountain
   Was all that he could see.
   Was all that he could see,
   Was all that he could see . . .

FUZZY WUZZY

Fuzzy Wuzzy was a bear.
Fuzzy Wuzzy had no hair.
Fuzzy Wuzzy wasn't fuzzy, was he?

Traditional

GRIZZLY BEAR*

Southern Work Song

1. I'm gon-na tell y'a lit-tle sto-ry 'bout a griz-zl-y bear,_

Tell y'a lit - tle sto - ry 'bout a griz - zl - y bear.

Well,_ a great big griz - zl - y, griz - zl - y bear,_

A great big griz - zl - y, griz - zl - y bear.

2. Well, my mama was a-scared of that grizzly bear,
   My mama was a-scared of that grizzly bear,
   So, my Daddy went a-huntin' for that grizzly bear,
   My Daddy went a-huntin' for that grizzly bear.

3. He had long, long hair that grizzly bear . . .
   He had big, blue eyes that grizzly bear . . .

4. Well, he looked everywhere for that grizzly bear . . .
   But he couldn't find that great big grizzly bear . . .

5. So, my mama's not a-scared of that grizzly bear . . .
   That great big grizzly, grizzly bear . . .

* This song is also sung as a call/response. Leader sings all but "grizzly bear" which group sings each time with enthusiasm.

At the Zoo

GOIN' TO THE ZOO

Pam Beall   *Traditional*

1. Oh, we're go-in' to the zoo, zoo, zoo_

To see the el-e-phants and wild kan-ga-roo,_

And while we are there,_ we'll see the po-lar bear,

'Cuz if we don't, we'll stay un-til we do._

2. Oh, we're goin' to the zoo, zoo, zoo
   To see the camels and the wild caribou,
   And while we are there, we'll see the panda bear*,
   'Cuz if we don't, we'll stay until we do.

3. Oh, we're goin' to the zoo, zoo, zoo
   To see the lions and the wild tigers, too,
   And while we are there, we'll see the grizzly bear,
   'Cuz if we don't, we'll stay until we do.

* The giant panda is bear-like but is actually not a bear.

AT THE ZOO

First I saw the white bear, then I saw the black;
Then I saw the camel with a hump upon his back;
Then I saw the grey wolf with mutton in his jaw;
Then I saw the wombat waddle in the straw;
Then I saw the elephant waving his long trunk;
Then I saw the monkeys—Eew! How they stunk!

William Makepeace Thackeray
1811–1863
(Adapted)

THE LION

Pam Beall   Saint-Saens

1. The li - on is the King of Beasts, He
roams a-round in Af - ri - ca, The an - i - mals on
which he feasts are an-te-lope and ze - bra.

2. The mighty roar the lion makes
   Fills all the animals with fright,
   I'm sure that when they see his face,
   They turn and run with all their might.

THE HIPPOPOTAMUS AND THE RHINOCEROS

Susan Nipp   *Traditional, adapted*

1. The hip-po-pot-a-mus__ and the rhi-noc-er-os__

Went for a walk one day, They saw a great big pud-dle and

jumped in the mid-dle, And they be-gan to play.

2. The hippopotamus and the rhinoceros
   Splashed and splashed all day,
   They turned that great big puddle right into a mud hole,
   And they began to say,
      (spoken) *"Ooey, gooey, mooshy, gooshy,
      What a perfect day!"*

THE OSTRICH

The ostrich is a funny bird,
He doesn't fly to travel
But runs quite fast on long, long legs
And eats green plants and gravel.

Susan Nipp

52

ONE ELEPHANT WENT OUT TO PLAY

Traditional

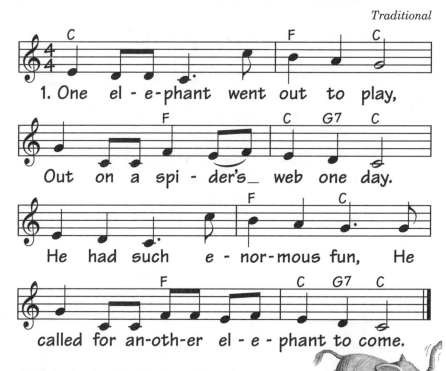

1. One el - e - phant went out to play,
Out on a spi - der's_ web one day.
He had such e - nor - mous fun, He
called for an - oth - er el - e - phant to come.

2. Two elephants went out to play . . .

3. Three elephants went out to play . . .

Game:

One child walks around the room like an elephant. At the end of the verse, he chooses another 'elephant' to join behind him. At the end of each verse, the last 'elephant' chosen selects a new 'elephant.' Continue until several children are imitating elephants.

THE ELEPHANT

The elephant carries a great big trunk;
He never packs it with clothes;
It has no lock and it has no key,
But he takes it wherever he goes.

Anonymous

THREE LITTLE MONKEYS
(Fingerplay)

Three little monkeys jumping on the bed,
(tap three fingers on palm of opposite hand)

One fell off and bumped his head.
(one finger falls off, then hold head)

Mama called the doctor and the doctor said,
(hold phone by ear, dial in air)

"No more little monkeys jumping on that bed."
(shake finger)

Repeat with "Two little monkeys . . . "
"One little monkey . . . "

FIVE LITTLE MONKEYS
(Fingerplay)

Five little monkeys
(hold up five fingers of one hand)

Swinging in a tree,
(swing hand side to side)

Teasing Mr. Alligator,
(wiggle fingers)

"Can't catch me!"
(continue wiggling fingers)

Along came Mr. Alligator,
(palms together, one on top of the other, fingers pointing outward, moving away from body)

Quiet as can be.
(continue moving hands forward)

SNAP!
(open hands, wrists still touching, then clap quickly together)

Repeat with "Four little monkeys . . . "
"Three . . . " "Two . . . " "One . . . "

THE MONKEY AND THE ZEBRA

Traditional

When the mon-key saw the ze-bra, He be-gan to switch his tail, "Well, I nev-er!" was his com-ment, "Here's a mule that's been to jail; Here's a mule that's been to jail, Here's a mule that's been to jail, Well, I nev-er!" was his com-ment, "Here's a mule that's been to jail!"

THE TIGER

There was a young lady of Niger,
Who smiled as she rode on a tiger;
They returned from the ride with the lady inside
And the smile on the face of the tiger.

Traditional

THE GIRAFFE

Susan Nipp   *Susan Nipp*

Have you ev-er looked a gi-raffe in the eye? It's a
dif-fi-cult thing to do,___ You must climb up high, way___
up in the sky___ or bend down low for a view,___ Be-cause it
munch-es on bunch-es of leaves in tall trees___ And
leans way down___ to get a drink from the ground,___ Be-cause it
munch-es on bunch-es of leaves in tall trees___ And
leans way down___ to get a drink from the ground.___

56

THE DUCK AND THE KANGAROO

Said the Duck to the Kangaroo,
"Good gracious! how you hop!
Over the fields and the water too,
As if you never would stop!
My life is a bore in this silly pond,
And I long to go out in the world beyond!
I wish I could hop like you!"
Said the Duck to the Kangaroo.

"Please give me a ride on your back!"
Said the Duck to the Kangaroo.
"I would sit quite still, and say nothing but 'Quack,'
The whole of the long day through!
And we'd go to the Dee, and the Jelly Bo Lee,
Over the land, and over the sea;
Please give me a ride! O do!"
Said the Duck to the Kangaroo.

Said the Kangaroo, "I'm ready!
All in the moonlight pale;
But to balance me well, dear Duck, sit steady!
And quite at the end of my tail!"
So away they went with a hop and a bound,
And they hopped the whole world three times round;
And who was so happy — O who,
As the Duck and the Kangaroo?

Edward Lear
1812–1888
Adapted

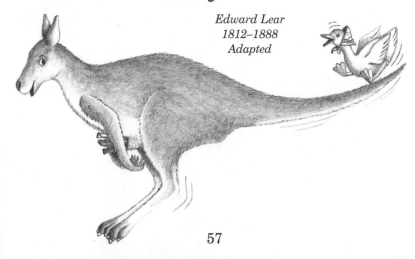

57

ANIMALS

Adapted, Pam Beall   *Traditional*

1. An - i - mals are big and an - i - mals are small,

We will sing this song and try to name them all.

2. Alligator, hedgehog, kangaroo, bear,
   Elephant, butterfly, porcupine, hare.

3. Kookaburra, camel, antelope, moose,
   Scorpion, dragonfly, parakeet, goose.

4. Salamander, zebra, ladybug, frog,
   Hummingbird, pelican, octopus, dog.

5. Caterpillar, reindeer, jellyfish, snail,
   Chickadee, polar bear, crocodile, quail.

6. Armadillo, donkey, caribou, skunk,
   Rattlesnake, cockatoo, buffalo, monk.

7. Animals are big and animals are small,
   Even though we tried, we didn't name them all!

Suggestion:
Try to sing each verse a little faster than the one before.

ANIMAL ACTION

Move to the rhythm, move to the beat,
Move your body and move your feet.

    Birds fly,
    Rabbits hop,
    Fish swim,
    Frogs kerplop!

    Ants march,
    Worms wiggle,
    Peacocks strut,
    Jellyfish jiggle.

Move to the rhythm, move to the beat,
Move your body and move your feet.

    Monkeys swing,
    Lions stalk,
    Eagles soar,
    People walk.

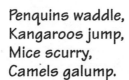

    Penquins waddle,
    Kangaroos jump,
    Mice scurry,
    Camels galump.

Move to the rhythm, move to the beat,
Move your body and move your feet.

Pam Beall

Actions: Move as words suggest

THE ANIMAL PARADE

(Tune: "The Washington Post" March)

Susan Nipp

John Philip Sousa, 1889

It's time for the big pa - rade of an - i - mals,__ They march to the left and to the right, They march all the day in-to the night, It's awe-some, this big pa - rade of an - i - mals, __ They march all a - round with won-der - ful sounds, It's such a de-light and quite a sight.

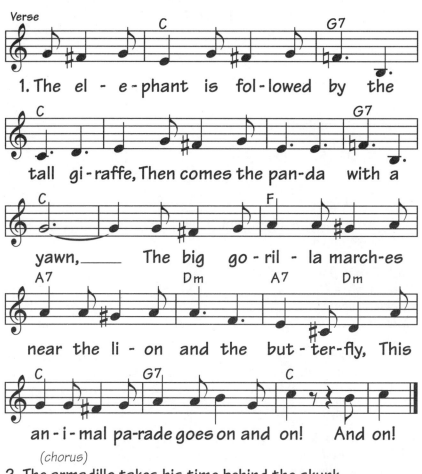

Verse

C   G7

1. The el - e - phant is fol - lowed by the

C   G7

tall gi - raffe, Then comes the pan - da with a

C   F

yawn, ___ The big go - ril - la march - es

A7   Dm   A7   Dm

near the li - on and the but - ter - fly, This

C   G7   C

an - i - mal pa - rade goes on and on! And on!

(chorus)

2. The armadillo takes his time behind the skunk,
   The shy koala rides a fawn,
   The parakeet flies by the peacock and the prickly porcupine,
   This animal parade goes on and on! And on!
   (chorus)

3. The rabbit hops between the frog and kangaroo,
   The penguin waddles by the swan,
   The ladybug and bumblebee fly high above the crocodile,
   This animal parade goes on and on! And on!

INDEX

Titles in italics are poems.
*Titles with asterisks are fingerplays.

Discover the entire best-selling line
of Wee Sing® books, audio, and videos

Book & Audiocassette packages
• Wee Sing Children's Songs and Fingerplays • Wee Sing and Play
• Wee Sing Silly Songs • Wee Sing Sing-Alongs
• Wee Sing for Christmas • Wee Sing Nursery Rhymes and Lullabies
• Wee Sing Bible Songs • Wee Sing America • Wee Sing Fun 'n' Folk
• Wee Sing Dinosaurs • Wee Sing Around the World
• Wee Sing More Bible Songs • Wee Sing for Baby
• Wee Sing Games, Games, Games • Wee Sing in the Car
• Wee Sing Animals, Animals, Animals • Wee Sing and Pretend
• Wee Sing 25th Anniversary Celebration • Wee Sing for Halloween

Book & CD (with FREE audiocassette) packages
• Wee Sing Children's Songs and Fingerplays • Wee Sing and Play
• Wee Sing Silly Songs • Wee Sing Sing-Alongs
• Wee Sing for Christmas • Wee Sing Nursery Rhymes and Lullabies
• Wee Sing Bible Songs • Wee Sing America • Wee Sing Fun 'n' Folk
• Wee Sing Dinosaurs • Wee Sing Around the World
• Wee Sing More Bible Songs • Wee Sing for Baby
• Wee Sing Games, Games, Games • Wee Sing in the Car
• Wee Sing Animals, Animals, Animals • Wee Sing and Pretend
• Wee Sing 25th Anniversary Celebration • Wee Sing for Halloween

Wee Sing® & Learn Book & Audiocassette packages
• Wee Sing & Learn ABC • Wee Sing & Learn 123
• Wee Sing & Learn Colors • Wee Sing & Learn Bugs
• Wee Sing & Learn Dinosaurs

Board Books
• The Hokey Pokey • Away in a Manger
• The Ten Days of Christmas • The Ants Go Marching
• If You're Happy and You Know It • Old MacDonald

Live-Action Videos
• Wee Sing Together • King Cole's Party • Grandpa's Magical Toys
• Wee Sing in Sillyville • The Best Christmas Ever!
• Wee Sing in the Big Rock Candy Mountains
• Wee Sing in the Marvelous Musical Mansion
• The Wee Sing Train • Wee Sing Under the Sea
• Animal Songs • Classic Songs for Kids • Wee Singdom

Also available
• The Wee Sing Musical Bible

**Wee Sing® products are available
wherever children's books and toys are sold.**